My Journey of Peace to Estonia, Latvia, Lithuania and Russia

My Journey of Peace to Estonia, Latvia, Lithuania and Russia

Tommy Koh

Ambassador-at-Large, Singapore

NEW JERSEY · LONDON · SINGAPORE · BEIJING · SHANGHAI · HONG KONG · TAIPEI · CHENNAI · TOKYO

Published by

World Scientific Publishing Co. Pte. Ltd.

5 Toh Tuck Link, Singapore 596224

USA office: 27 Warren Street, Suite 401-402, Hackensack, NJ 07601

UK office: 57 Shelton Street, Covent Garden, London WC2H 9HE

National Library Board, Singapore Cataloguing in Publication Data
Name(s): Koh, Tommy T. B. (Tommy Thong Bee), 1937–
Title: My journey of peace to Estonia, Latvia, Lithuania and Russia / Tommy Koh.
Description: Singapore : World Scientific Publishing Co. Pte. Ltd., [2025]
Identifier(s): ISBN 978-981-12-9856-1 (hardcover) | ISBN 978-981-98-0075-9 (paperback) |
    ISBN 978-981-12-9857-8 (ebook for institutions) |
    ISBN 978-981-12-9858-5 (ebook for individuals)
Subject(s): LCSH: Koh, Tommy T. B. (Tommy Thong Bee), 1937– |
    Baltic States--Foreign relations--Russia (Federation) |
    Russia (Federation)--Foreign relations--Baltic States. |
    Baltic States--Politics and government--1991– |
    Russia (Federation)--Politics and government--1991–
Classification: DDC 327.479047--dc23

British Library Cataloguing-in-Publication Data
A catalogue record for this book is available from the British Library.

For any available supplementary material, please visit
https://www.worldscientific.com/worldscibooks/10.1142/13996#t=suppl

Desk Editor: Jiang Yulin

Typeset by Stallion Press
Email: enquiries@stallionpress.com

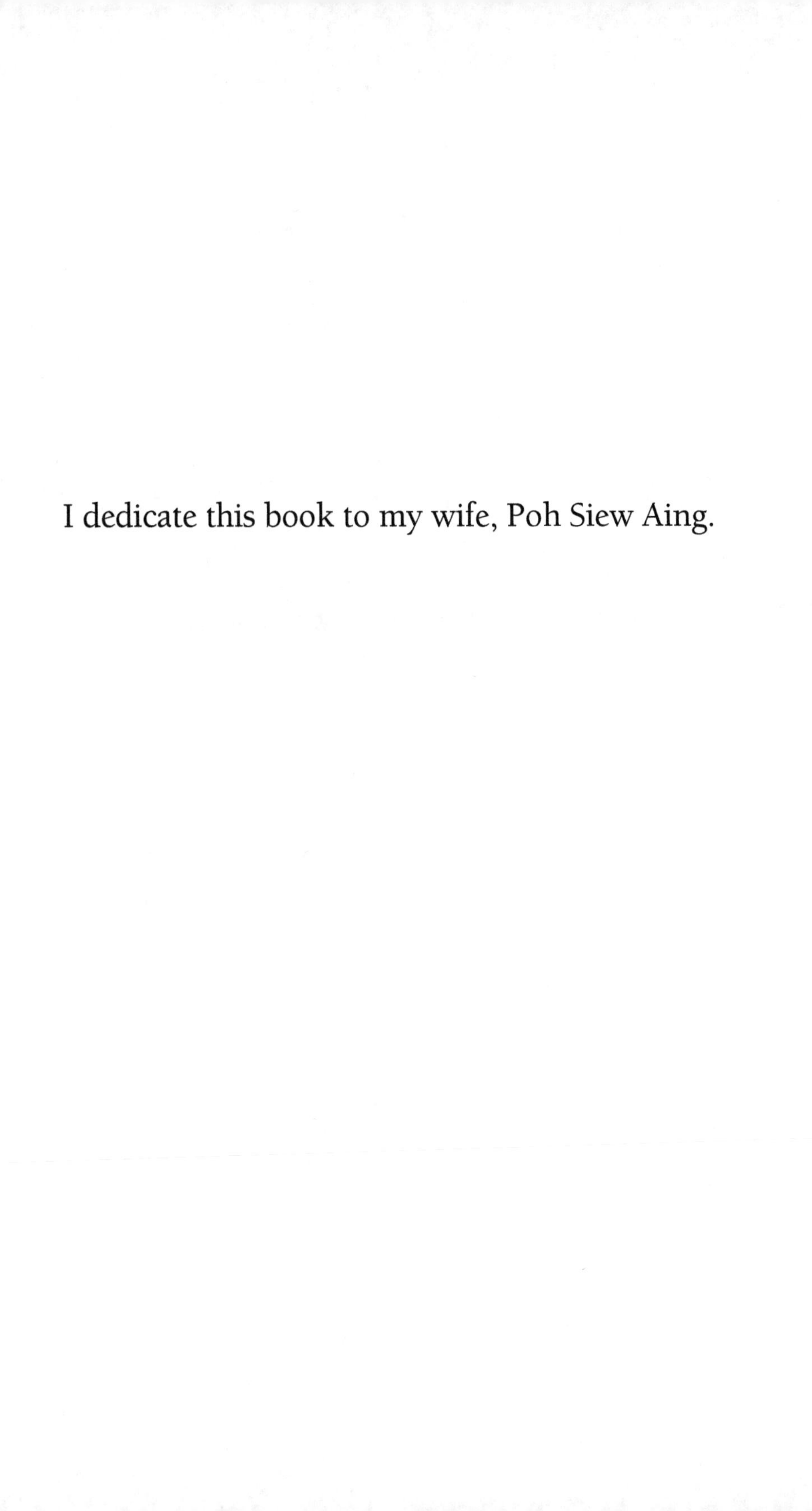

I dedicate this book to my wife, Poh Siew Aing.

Content

Maps   ix
Foreword by Ambassador Priit Turk   xiii
Foreword by Ambassador Normans Penke   xvii
Foreword by Ambassador Darius Gaidys   xxi
Preface   xxiii

Chapter 1   The End of the Cold War   1
Chapter 2   The United Nations   5
Chapter 3   Preparing for Moscow   9
Chapter 4   Visit to Lithuania   13
Chapter 5   Visit to Latvia   19
Chapter 6   Visit to Estonia   25
Chapter 7   Return to Moscow   33
Chapter 8   Report to the United Nations Secretary-General and the General Assembly   41
Chapter 9   Reflections   43

Annex A: United Nations General Assembly
      Resolution 47/21   47
Annex B: Report of the Good Offices Mission to
      Estonia, Latvia, Lithuania and the
      Russian Federation   51
Index   73

Maps

Russia

Estonia

Latvia

Lithuania

Foreword I

31st of August 2024 marks 30 years since Estonia was finally freed from 50 years of occupying troops of the Soviet Union/Russian Federation. Real independence and sovereignty of Estonia was restored again and the Second World War finally finished for us.

In the face of Russia's current aggressive and imperialistic stance, the importance of the agreement for swift withdrawal of Russian military from Estonian soil cannot be overstated. It paved the way for subsequent steps to use our window of opportunity to integrate with the West by applying and joining the European Union and the North Atlantic Treaty Organization (NATO) — safeguarding Estonia's independent future.

Had the Russian forces remained until 2002 or beyond as proposed by Russian government at the time, the trajectory of Estonia's development could have been drastically different. The 2008 war in Georgia, 2014 war and annexation of Crimea and East Ukraine and today's war against the very existence of Ukraine as a country have proven to everyone that Russian imperialist goals and lack of any respect to international law are not only existential threats to any neighbouring nation, but also to broader international security.

In the early years of Estonia's re-independence and during negotiations with the Russian Federation, Estonia could not do it without strong international support, especially from our Western allies and particularly the United States. Their backing and help to convince Russia to withdraw the troops by the end of August 1994, at the same time Russia did from unified Germany and other Baltic countries, was crucial for the future progress.

Furthermore, the broader international community already expressed in 1993 through a General Assembly resolution very clear and unanimous support for the timely, orderly and complete withdrawal of foreign forces from Estonia and Latvia (a deal with Lithuania was already reached).

Ambassador Tommy Koh is a globally known and highly respected diplomat for his contribution and unwavering commitment to international law. I was also one of those persons who learned about his important role as the

United Nations (UN) Secretary-General Special Envoy to Baltic countries during those crucial times for Estonia only when preparing to become the Ambassador of Estonia to Singapore.

Despite his initial unfamiliarity with the region, Ambassador Koh's staunch belief in the equal rights of all states and his prior experience in international roles, including the chair of negotiations of the Law of the Sea, made him, as the voice of the international community, well respected and instrumental.

His personal commitment and contribution to Estonia's future is also a symbolic foundation for close Estonia–Singapore relations and deep mutual understanding today. "Singapore, Estonia we think alike" as said by President Tharman during his first ever presidential visit of a Singaporean president to Estonia in June 2024. Ambassador Tommy Koh and our countries believe deeply and speak out for the protection and respect of international law and the UN Charter. Always. We need these voices to be heard now more than ever before.

I am honoured to have known Ambassador Tommy Koh and am continually inspired by his stories of international law in the making and how small countries can be instrumental in shaping international law and protecting their interests.

His decision to document those turbulent times and to counter false Russian narratives about NATO enlargement or justifications of spheres of influence is commendable and highly necessary.

Priit Turk
Estonian Ambassador to Singapore,
Indonesia and ASEAN

Foreword II

Time passes, and memories filled with emotions and in good faith tend to deviate and naturally must acquire another perspective. It is said that history is written by the winners. In contrast, Professor Tommy Koh's book is a fine example of personal reflection rooted in facts. More like a diary of events, the writing inspires the reader to search for further information. It is my honour and privilege to be invited by Professor Tommy Koh to be among the select few to read his reflection first-hand.

The ties in the early 1990s between Latvians, Estonians, and Lithuanians were historically tough and crucial for our statehood—sovereignty and independence. One of the first decisions by the Parliament of Latvia in 1991 was on the complete withdrawal of Soviet armed forces from Latvia. It was clear that for an independent, sovereign country, it would be totally unacceptable to have any Russian soldier on our soil. Memories of our own painful history were still very much alive. Just for the readers to remember — in

1939 a treaty on non-aggression between Nazi Germany and the Soviet Union (USSR), also known as Hitler–Stalin pact, was signed. According to the secret protocols of the pact, the two dictators agreed on zones of influence, that is, specifying which territories would be occupied. Thus, the USSR succeeded in opening military bases in three Baltic states, laying the foundation for the subsequent occupation of three independent nations in 1940. Certainly, there were no second thoughts about the destiny of Soviet troops on our soil in 1991 — they had to leave.

Although Latvia is a relatively small country (about 64,000 square kilometres) and one might suppose that withdrawing Soviet armed forces would be a relatively easy task, this was far from the truth. Not only did political difficulties lie ahead but also logistical ones as well. During the occupation of Latvia, 12 ballistic missile launch sites and 22 airfields were built, 60,000 military personnel were present, and 3,009 military units were deployed in more than 700 locations including navy bases in three major ports.

As a young diplomat, I was on the Latvian negotiation team. I remember that when our political leaders finally saw the classified Soviet files listing all the military constructions and personnel attached — they, along the whole negotiation team, were aghast by the magnitude of the "contamination". It could easily be said that every third person you met in Latvia at that time was in one way or another linked to the Soviet military. The stakes were high. Unquestionably, the goal could not be achieved without enormous help from the United States, Sweden, and international organisations — the United Nations, the Organization for Security and Co-operation in Europe, and many good friends from all around the world.

The talks lasted 26 months, during which 13 meetings were held. Finally, the agreement was signed in Moscow on the 30th of April 1994 by President of the Russian Federation Boris Yeltsin, President of Latvia Guntis Ulmanis, and Prime Minister Valdis Birkavs.

The last Russian military aircraft took off from Riga Airport and left Latvian airspace at 18:00, 31 August 1994.

The nature of our world will always push mankind further in its quest for a better life. Yet to build our future, it is imperative that we study our past. Lessons learned throughout history should help guide us in structuring the world around us. The brutality, cruelness, and ongoing wars still faced in too many places of the world suggest otherwise and that perhaps one has not been taught well in school.

I am thankful for Professor Tommy Koh, Singapore's Ambassador-at-Large, eminent diplomat, and international lawyer for his crucial contribution and personal efforts during the Soviet troop withdrawal from the Baltics as well as the publication of his memories. Compelling and insightful!

Normans Penke
Non-resident Ambassador of Latvia to Indonesia,
Malaysia and Singapore

Foreword III

I am honored to write a few words about the new book by the prominent Singaporean diplomat and lawyer, Professor Tommy Koh. This book provides an insightful account of the events and meetings that led to a lesser-known historical fact: the withdrawal of Russian troops from the three Baltic states. This withdrawal marked the end of World War II for Lithuania, Latvia, and Estonia.

At that time, I was a young Lithuanian diplomat stationed at the Consulate-General in New York. While I cannot personally attest to the celebrations in Lithuania, the vivid memories shared by my family, colleagues, and friends confirm that the withdrawal of Russian troops brought immense joy, happiness, and optimism.

This book is an invaluable resource for historians, diplomats, and anyone interested in the turbulent history of the 20th century in the Baltics.

Darius Gaidys
Ambassador of Lithuania to Singapore

Preface

Two events motivated me to write this book.

First, the President of Singapore, Tharman Shanmugaratnam, made a state visit to Estonia from 25 to 26 June 2024. Before his visit, I asked him whether he was aware of my visit to Estonia in 1993 as the United Nations (UN) Secretary-General's Special Envoy. He replied in the negative. In view of his answer, I felt that I should write a book about my UN assignment to help the three Baltic countries, Estonia, Latvia and Lithuania, come to an agreement with Russia on the withdrawal of Russian troops from their territories and other related matters.

Second, Russia's invasion of Ukraine on 24 February 2022 caused alarm bells to ring very loudly in the three Baltic countries. It brought back many bad memories of how Russia had invaded and occupied their countries and incorporated them into the Russian Empire. Although they are members of the North Atlantic Treaty Organization and should feel secure, they nevertheless feel threatened by an aggressive and expansionist Russia under President Vladimir Putin.

It is for these two reasons that I have decided to tell my story. I hope readers will enjoy reading this small book.

I would like to record my gratitude to three friends who have passed away. The first is Dr Boutros Boutros-Ghali who appointed me as his Special Envoy. The second is Mr Paul Koh Kok Hong, a good friend and colleague. He looked after me during my two visits to Moscow in 1993. The third is Ambassador Tom Pickering, the US Ambassador in Moscow. Without his help, I would have been unable to get inside the Kremlin to meet with a senior member of President Boris Yeltsin's staff.

Chapter 1

The End of the Cold War

During the Second World War, the United States, the United Kingdom and Russia were allies. The alliance was based on the fact that they had a common enemy, Nazi Germany. When Germany was defeated, the alliance ended and the three countries went their separate ways.

In 1945, the victorious Russian Army had troops in many Central and Eastern European countries. With the help of local communist parties, they managed to seize power in those countries. Moscow incorporated them into the Russian Empire, known as the Union of Soviet Socialist Republics (USSR), or the Soviet Union for short.

Latvia became the Latvian Soviet Socialist Republic. Estonia became the Estonian Soviet Socialist Republic and Lithuania became the Lithuanian Soviet Socialist Republic. They would remain as part of the Russian Empire until 1991, when the USSR was dissolved and they became free.

Let me describe briefly the histories of the three Baltic countries. Estonia had been ruled by Germany, Denmark, Sweden and Russia. In 1918, at the end of the First World War, Estonia became an independent state. When the Second World War began, Estonia declared a policy of neutrality. This, however, did not save Estonia from being fought over by Germany and Russia. In 1944, Estonia was occupied by the Soviet Union. It was incorporated into the USSR as the Estonian Soviet Socialist Republic. Estonia regained its independence in 1991 when the USSR was dissolved.

Like Estonia, Latvia was also ruled by many foreign rulers, such as Germany, Sweden, Polish-Lithuanian Commonwealth and Russia. Latvia became independent in 1918 at the end of World War One. In 1944, Latvia was occupied by the Soviet Union and was incorporated into the USSR as the Latvian Soviet Socialist Republic. It regained its independence in 1991.

Lithuania's historical journey is different from those of Estonia and Latvia. The Kingdom of Lithuania was established in 1253. In 1569, Lithuania merged with Poland to form the Polish-Lithuanian Commonwealth. In 1795, most of the territory of Lithuania was annexed by Russia. In 1918, Lithuania became independent. In 1944, it was incorporated into the USSR as the Lithuanian Soviet Socialist Republic. In 1990, one year before the dissolution of the Soviet Union, Lithuania issued a declaration of independence.

The 41 years during which Estonia, Latvia and Lithuania were ruled by the Russians were very difficult years. They were forbidden from speaking their own languages and had to learn to communicate in Russian. To overcome this prohibition, they took up singing. By doing so, they kept their national languages alive. They also produced world-class choirs. As the then chairman of the National Arts Council, I invited two of them to perform in Singapore at our annual Singapore International Arts Festival in 1994 and 1996.

Many Estonians and Latvians were banished to Siberia because they had opposed Russian rule. Many of them died in their exile because of the extreme climate and harsh conditions. As a result of these bitter experiences, the hatred of Russia and Russians was palpable in Estonia and Latvia.

In 1991, there were Russian troops in all three Baltic countries. In addition, there were Russian bases in Estonia and Latvia. Estonia, Latvia and Lithuania demanded the immediate withdrawal of the Russian troops and the closure of the Russian bases. The Russians pleaded for time.

Russia appointed three chief negotiators, one for each Baltic country. The three Baltic countries each appointed a chief negotiator to negotiate with Russia.

The negotiations were protracted and not successful. The main problem was the absence of trust and goodwill. In their absence, compromise was elusive.

Estonia, Latvia and Lithuania decided to refer their disputes with Russia to the United Nations General Assembly.

Chapter 2

The United Nations

The 47th session of the United Nations (UN) General Assembly in 1993 considered the demands of the three Baltic countries for the complete withdrawal of Russian troops from their territories. At the end of the debate, the General Assembly adopted, without a vote, Resolution 47/21 (see Annex A).

Resolution 47/21 called upon all states concerned "to conclude without delay appropriate agreement, including timetables, for the early, orderly and complete withdrawal of foreign military forces from the territories of Estonia, Latvia and Lithuania".

In the same resolution, the General Assembly urged the Secretary-General to use his good offices to facilitate the complete withdrawal of foreign military forces from the territories of Estonia, Latvia and Lithuania.

The UN Secretary-General in 1993 was Egyptian Dr Boutros Boutros-Ghali. He liked the way in which I had chaired the Preparatory Committee for the 1992 UN Conference on Environment and Development (Earth Summit) and the negotiations at the Summit in Rio, Brazil. He asked me to join his cabinet in New York. I declined his kind offer.

I told him that there was a conflict of interest when chairing a UN conference and then taking up a job in the UN Secretariat on the same subject. I explained that in 1982, the then Secretary-General, Javiér Perez de Cuéllar, had also offered me a job in his cabinet after I had chaired the UN Conference on the Law of the Sea. I had also declined his offer for the same reason. Dr Boutros-Ghali said that he did not see any conflict of interest but accepted my decision.

In 1993, I received a telephone call from Dr Boutros-Ghali. He told me about UN General Assembly Resolution 47/21. He said that he would like to appoint me as his Special Envoy. I was surprised by his offer. I told him that I was not qualified for the job as I had never been to the four countries. He said that that was good as I carried no baggage from the past. The Singapore Government urged me to accept the appointment on the ground that Singapore should try to be relevant and useful to the world. I therefore accepted appointment as the UN Secretary-General's Special Envoy, with the rank of an Under-Secretary-General.

What is the role of the Special Envoy? I interpreted my role as a combination of mediation and conciliation. I had to gain the trust of the four countries. I had to understand the interests and positions of the four countries. I had to be impartial and objective. I had to try to narrow the gaps between them by putting forward compromises which all sides could live with.

Before proceeding to New York to be briefed by the UN, I spent several weeks reading about the histories of the three Baltic countries and their relations with their neighbours. Why is it important to read about their histories? The reason is that, very often, you cannot understand the present if you do not know the past. I have come to the conclusion that history never dies. Many contemporary problems have deep historical roots.

Secretary-General Boutros Boutros-Ghali and I sharing a light-hearted moment during my chairing of a Preparatory Committee meeting for the Earth Summit. After the Secretary-General accidentally read the same page twice, I stopped him and told him that he need not pay the same compliment twice. Only then he realised his mistake, and everyone had a good laugh.

In 1993, Dr Boutros-Ghali appointed me as his Special Envoy to resolve the withdrawal of Russian armed forces in Estonia, Latvia and Lithuania.

Chapter 3

Preparing for Moscow

I was informed by the United Nations (UN) that I would be assisted by three persons. Ms Lynda Smith, a UN official from the United Kingdom (UK), would be the Secretary of the delegation. Mr Alexandre Matsuoka, a member of the UN Secretariat from Ukraine, would be my political adviser. Colonel Stanislav Hajek, from the General Staff of the Czech Republic, would be my military adviser.

I was briefed by Dr Boutros Boutros-Ghali before I departed New York for Moscow. He was a brilliant man but very blunt and direct. He told me to tell the leaders of Estonia, Latvia and Lithuania that they should be more flexible because it was their destiny to live next to Russia, and that while Russia was weak in 1993, it would be strong again in future. I thanked him for his advice and added that I would convey his point, but in a more tactful manner.

Whilst in New York, I met with the diplomatic representatives of Estonia, Latvia, Lithuania, Russia, Denmark, Finland,

Germany, Poland, Sweden and the United States (US). I explained my mission to them and asked for their advice and support. All of them assured me of their support.

On Sunday, 29 August 1993, Mr Matsuoka, Ms Smith and I arrived in Moscow in the late afternoon. Colonel Hajek was waiting for us at the airport. A friend from the Singapore Embassy, Paul Koh Kok Hong, was also at the airport to receive me. Instead of taking us to our hotel, our Russian host took us to visit a military camp, Solnechnogorsk, some distance from Moscow.

When we arrived at the military camp, we were greeted by Lieutenant General Igor Puzanov, the first Deputy Commander of the Moscow Military District. I was given a guided tour of the camp. I saw for myself that the troops and their families, recently withdrawn from Lithuania, were living in tents. I expressed my sympathy and said that I understood Russia's position, that it needed time to build housing for the returning troops and their families.

At the end of the visit, I asked General Puzanov whether I could have a cup of hot tea. He said that he had prepared a small reception for me. The table in the reception room was laden with food and caviar. He stood up and proposed a toast to me with vodka. It was bottoms up. In accordance with the Russian custom, I had to respond with a toast to him.

After several rounds of toasting, my friend Paul Koh came up to me and asked if I was feeling okay. I told him that, thanks to my parents' genes, I was still sober. My Secretary, Lynda Smith, was knocked out by the lethal spirit, vodka.

On Monday, 30 August 1993, we went to the Ministry of Foreign Affairs of the Russian Federation. We met with the Head of the European Department, Mr Glukhov, and Mr Boris Nikolaevich Krylov, the Secretary-General and Chief of Chancery.

We also met with the three chief negotiators. The Chief Negotiator for Latvia was Ambassador Sergei Zotov. The Chief Negotiator for Lithuania was Ambassador Virgilijus Isakov and the Chief Negotiator for Estonia was Ambassador Vasili Svirin. All three of them complained about the unreasonable attitude of their Baltic counterparts. There was clearly no trust and no goodwill between them.

We called on the Deputy Defence Minister, Colonel General Boris Gromov, a celebrated soldier. He was decorated for his bravery in Afghanistan.

On Tuesday, 31 August 1993, we met Mr Sergei Stepashin, the Chairman of the Commission on Defence and Security of the Russian Parliament.

We also met with the ambassadors of Belgium, Denmark, Greece and the US. The US Ambassador, Tom Pickering, was an old friend. It was a good fortune for me that he was in Moscow.

We flew from Moscow to Vilnius, the capital of Lithuania, in a Russian military aircraft made available to us by Colonel General Gromov. It was very kind of him to accede to my request as no commercial flight was available.

Joining me in my peace mission were (from left to right) Colonel Stanislav Hajek, General Staff of the Czech Republic, who was my military adviser; Mr Alexandre Matsuoka, a member of the UN Secretariat from Ukraine, who was my political adviser; and Ms Lynda Smith, a UN official from the UK, who was the Secretary of the delegation.

Chapter 4

Visit to Lithuania

I will never forget 31 August 1993. We arrived in Vilnius in the late afternoon. The Chief of Protocol of Lithuania was at the airport to receive us. He looked exceptionally happy. He said that instead of taking us to our hotel, he was taking us to the square in front of the Parliament.

We arrived at Parliament Square and witnessed people full of joy and happiness. I asked the Chief of Protocol what they were celebrating. He said that they were celebrating the departure of the last Russian combat soldier from Lithuania. I was introduced to Professor Vytautas Landsbergis, the music professor who had founded Sąjūdis and had campaigned for Lithuania's independence.

From Parliament Square, we were taken to the President's Palace, where there was more rejoicing. The next day, we met with President Algirdas Brazauskas. We asked him to explain what had happened the day before. President

Brazauskas was the head of the Communist Party of Lithuania before independence. After independence, he stood for election and was elected as the first post-independence President. He explained that he was a fake communist, and the people understood that he had done it in order to protect his country.

President Brazauskas told us that on 30 August, he had phoned his friend "Comrade Boris" in Moscow. He had told the Russian leader that the "UN man" was coming to Lithuania on 31 August and had requested President Boris Yeltsin to pull out his remaining troops on 31 August. President Yeltsin agreed.

I asked President Brazauskas whether he could call "Comrade Boris" again and ask him to withdraw his troops from Estonia and Latvia. The President laughed and said that he could not do so.

I found out that the Lithuanian National Symphony Orchestra was performing on the evening of 1 September. I asked President Brazauskas whether they could help us purchase four tickets for the concert. He said that we could sit in the President's box in the symphony hall. That evening, many Lithuanians at the concert must have wondered who was the Asian man sitting in the President's box.

We also met with the Foreign Minister, Mr Povilas Gylys; his deputy, Mr Virginijus Domarkas and the members of the delegation negotiating with Russia. They were Professor Virgilijus Vladislovas Bulovas, Mr R Ozolas and Professor Vadapalas. With the departure of the Russian troops, their job was done.

In Vilnius, we met with representatives of the Russian war veterans and retirees. They told us that they wished to return to Russia. They complained that their government was not helping them to do so. We promised to put in a good word for them in Moscow.

We also met with the diplomatic corps in Vilnius. We briefed them on our mission and asked for their support.

We travelled by car from Vilnius to Riga, the capital of Latvia. The distance was about 290 kilometres and the journey took about three-and-a-half hours. We left Lithuania with great satisfaction, knowing that our mission was accomplished. We wondered what lay ahead for us in Latvia and Estonia.

Visiting a military camp at Solnechnogorsk, on the outskirts of Moscow. Joining me in this visit was Paul Koh (standing on far left), who was with the Singapore Embassy in Moscow. Hosted by Lieutenant General Igor Puzanov (standing on my right), this trip allowed me to witness first-hand the living conditions of the military personnel and their families who had returned from Lithuania. I understood from the visit that Russia needed time to build housing for the returning troops and their families.

At the end of our tour around the Solnechnogorsk military camp, Lieutenant General Puzanov (right) and I toasted over vodka in accordance with a Russian custom. Due to my parents' good genes, I passed my vodka test.

Meeting the three chief negotiators and their boss (standing from left to right: Ambassador S. Zotov, Chief Negotiator for Latvia; Y. E. Fokine, head of the Second European Department; Ambassador V. Isakov, Chief Negotiator for Lithuania; Ambassador V. Svirin, Chief Negotiator for Estonia).

Chapter 5

Visit to Latvia

We arrived in Riga, the beautiful capital of Latvia, on the morning of 3 September 1993. In the afternoon, we called on the President of Latvia, Mr Guntis Ulmanis. He told us that he supported our mission.

We then met with the Foreign Minister, Professor Georgs Andrejevs, and the members of the Latvian delegation negotiating with Russia. They were Ambassador Mārtiņš Virsis, Mr A Vovers, Colonel D Turlais and Mr M Supe. We discussed the sticking points in their negotiations with Russia and possible compromises.

On that evening, we met with the Dean of the diplomatic corps, Count Alexandre Graf of Germany. He was very knowledgeable about Russia and shared his insights with us. We would have preferred meeting with the whole diplomatic corps and not just the Dean.

On Saturday, 4 September, we spent the morning at the Latvian Parliament. We met with the Chairman of the Human Rights Committee, Ms. I Birzniece; the Chairman of the Foreign Relations Committee, Mr A Kirsteins; the Chairman of the Defence and Interior Committee, Mr I Silars, and the Chairman of the Committee on National Security, Mr A Pantelejevs.

The members of the Latvian Parliament were very anti-Russia. They were not receptive to my narrative that they should forgive Russia and put the past behind them. They were also not sympathetic to my plea that they should treat the Russian veterans and retirees in Latvia with kindness. My argument was that if the retirees were badly treated, a future Russian government could use them as a weapon against Latvia.

We also met with the Russian Lieutenant General Melnichuk, the Deputy Commander of the North-West Military Group. We met separately with representatives of the Russian veterans and retirees. Unlike the situation in Lithuania, those in Latvia would like to remain in Latvia. They requested me to plead their case with the Latvian Government. I agreed to do so. I felt that the veterans and retirees should be allowed to stay. I also felt that the Latvian Government should not take away their housing and healthcare.

On Sunday, 5 September, we flew to Liepaja in a Latvian military aircraft to inspect the Russian naval base. Moscow had described the naval base as a strategic facility. It wanted a lease of five to six years. When we met Captain Stalev, the Commander of the base, he told us that the Commander of the Baltic Fleet had drawn up a timetable for the withdrawal of the Russian Navy from Liepaja by the end of 1994. Moscow had not told us the truth.

After Liepaja, we visited Skrunda. In the 1960s, the Russians had built an anti-ballistic missile (ABM) early warning system in Skrunda. According to the Russian commander, Skrunda covered a section of the sky not covered by any other ABM early warning system in Russia or Ukraine. Therefore, he argued that, if Skrunda were to shut down, it would leave a hole in the sky. I verified the accuracy of this statement with the Americans. What the Russians wanted from Latvia was a special lease to continue to operate the facility or sufficient time for Russia to build a similar facility inside Russia.

Because of the shortage of time, we were unable to visit another Russian facility in Ventspils. According to Russia, the facility was to monitor objects in space. The Latvians felt that its purpose was to eavesdrop on communications in Northern Europe, especially the Scandinavian countries. The Russians asked for a lease of six years. The Latvians wanted it to be shut down immediately.

Before leaving Latvia for Estonia, we felt that it would be possible for Latvia and Russia to arrive at agreements on all the three issues if the two sides had the political will to agree, if Latvia was prepared to put its painful past behind it, if Russia were prepared to treat Latvia as a sovereign and independent state, and if both sides shared the vision to build a new future based on equality, mutual benefit and good neighbourliness.

We flew from Riga to the capital of Estonia, Tallinn.

Calling on the President of Latvia, Guntis Ulmanis (standing third from left).

Visiting a naval base in Liepaja, Latvia, hosted by commander of the base Captain Stalev. I was informed that the Commander of Russia's Baltic Fleet had already planned to withdraw his fleet by end-1994, which was earlier than the date given to us in Moscow.

Chapter 6

Visit to Estonia

Tallinn, the capital of Estonia, is a beautiful city. It is located near Saint Petersburg, Russia and Helsinki, Finland. Culturally, Estonia and Finland are very close and their languages are mutually comprehensible.

The people of Estonia, like the Latvians, hated Russia. This was because Stalin had banished a large segment of the Estonian intelligentsia to Siberia. Many of them perished. The then President of Estonia, Mr Lennart Meri, was one of the survivors. I understood how they felt but tried, in a gentle way, to persuade them to forgive the Russians and to put the past behind them.

In our two days in Tallinn, we met with the Prime Minister, Mr Mart Laar; the Minister of Defence, Mr Jüri Luik; the Minister of Foreign Affairs, Mr Trivimi Velliste; the Minister for the Environment, Mr Andres Tarand; the General Commander of the Defence Forces, Major General Aleksander Einseln; the Speaker of the Estonian

Parliament, Mr Ülo Nugis; the Chairman of the Foreign Affairs Committee of the Parliament, Mr Saatpalu; the General-Secretary of the Ministry of Foreign Affairs, Mr A Ollium; and the Head of the Political Department in the Ministry of Foreign Affairs, Mr T Miller.

There were between 5,000 and 6,000 Russian troops in Estonia. Russia would only agree to withdraw the troops if the two sides could conclude a binding legal agreement. Russia also linked troop withdrawal to two other issues: (a) the status and social benefits of Russian veterans and retirees and (b) an agreement on the Russian base in Paldiski.

We visited the Russian submarine training centre in Paldiski. There were two nuclear-powered submarines at the centre. The nuclear reactors had been deactivated. The questions which the two sides could not agree on were: (a) how long it would take Russia to remove the nuclear fuel rods from the two reactors, (b) how long it would take Russia to move the nuclear waste to storage and (c) how long it would take Russia to remove the reactors and other military secrets and clean up the site ecologically. The issues were technical and not political. Given goodwill, it should not be difficult to arrive at a reasonable compromise.

One of the highlights of our visit to Tallinn was the invitation to lunch by President Meri at his official residence. He was a wise man. He supported my mission but warned me that I would have a tough time in my meetings with the Estonian Parliament.

During the lunch, President Meri told us his story. His parents had opposed Russian rule of Estonia. They were banished to Siberia. He grew up in Siberia and survived the ordeal. He studied in Moscow and became a journalist. In order to make a living he had to join the All Soviet-Journalists Union, which he did.

In those days, when a Soviet leader was going to visit a foreign country, the government would ask the Journalists Union whether any journalists would be interested to join the delegation. President Meri said that visits to the West were always over-subscribed.

One day, the Journalists Union was told that a Soviet leader was going to visit Burma. Mr Meri was the only journalist who offered to join the delegation. His offer was accepted.

When they arrived at the airport in Rangoon, they were received by the Burmese Chief of Protocol. Each member of the Soviet delegation was introduced to him. When it was Mr Meri's turn to be introduced, he whispered something in the ear of the Burmese Chief of Protocol which made the latter very excited. The Burmese Chief of Protocol then shouted a command and a police officer promptly arrived and escorted Mr Meri away. The Soviet delegation thought he was defecting and protested.

What Mr Meri said to the Burmese Chief of Protocol was that he was from Estonia and he would like to visit the two Estonian priests, one of whom was Fredrich V Lustig, at the Shwedagon Pagoda. The police escorted him to the famous pagoda, where he had a warm reunion with the two Estonian Buddhist priests. The priests were in touch with the Estonian diaspora. Such news was censored and not available in the Soviet Union.

On the date of the withdrawal of Russian troops from Estonia, the gap in the schedule was not great. Estonia wanted them out by the end of 1993. Russia proposed the end of 1994. The Estonians offered to join a multi-national effort to build housing for the returning troops in Russia. Having seen the terrible conditions under which the returning troops and their families were housed, I pleaded with the Estonian leaders to give Russia more time to withdraw their troops.

The status and social benefits of Russian veterans and retirees was a difficult question. Unlike the situation in Lithuania, the Russians in Estonia would have liked to remain and not return to Russia. The Estonians would have preferred all of them to return to Russia. The number of veterans and retirees was quite large, approximately 52,000. They were afraid they would be expelled from Estonia.

When I met with the representatives of the Russian veterans and retirees, I told them that I would plead their case with the Estonian authorities. They were very grateful. One retired Russian General said that, if he were not an atheist, he would ask God to bless me. I thanked him anyway for his kind thought.

I told the Russian community that if they wanted to become Estonian citizens, they should be loyal to Estonia, learn its language and respect its culture. I told them that they could no longer expect to enjoy special rights and privileges. They should, however, be treated with fairness and humanity.

They told me of their fear that, under the Law of Aliens, they could be expelled from Estonia. I raised their fear with Prime Minister Laar. He told me that a decree would be enacted under the Aliens Law to exempt all who were over the age of 60. As for the cut-off date, I suggested to the Prime Minister to use the date on which Estonia gained its independence.

I urged Prime Minister Laar to treat the Russian veterans and retirees with kindness. I said that if they were treated with kindness, they would be loyal to Estonia. If, on the other hand, they were treated unfairly, they would be resentful, and they could be used by Russia to destabilise Estonia. I urged the Prime Minister not to take away their housing and healthcare benefits.

From Tallinn, we flew to Moscow.

Visiting Riigikogu, the Parliament of Estonia, to meet leaders of the Estonian Parliament.

Visiting a Russian nuclear submarine training school in Paldiski, Estonia. The issues were technical in nature, primarily dealing with the safe removal and disposal of nuclear rods and reactors at the site.

Hosted to lunch by President of Estonia Lennart Meri (sixth from left) at his official residence. Meri and his family were banished to Siberia. He survived the ordeal.

The delegation and our escort standing in front of the Alexander Nevsky Cathedral in Tallinn, Estonia.

Chapter 7

Return to Moscow

We returned to Moscow on 7 September. On 8 September, we went back to the Russian Ministry of Foreign Affairs and met with the three Russian Chief Negotiators.

We had a separate meeting with Mr Y E Fokine, the Head of the Second European Department. I think the Chief Negotiators reported to Mr Fokine.

We called on the Deputy Foreign Minister, Mr Vitaly Churkin. I had met him when we both served in our respective embassies in Washington. We briefed our Russian interlocutors on our visits to Estonia, Latvia and Lithuania. We reviewed the unresolved issues in their negotiations with the three Baltic countries. We also suggested some possible compromises.

Friends who are knowledgeable about Russia had told me that, in Russia, power is concentrated in the President. I was told that it was essential for me to see a senior person on President Boris Yeltsin's staff in the Kremlin. I asked the United Nations (UN) Secretary-General to get me such an appointment but he failed. I asked the Singapore Ambassador in Moscow to try but he also failed.

The person who came to my rescue was the United States (US) Ambassador in Moscow, Ambassador Tom Pickering. I told him of my dilemma. He told me that he would use his contacts inside the Kremlin to get me an appointment.

A few hours later, the Singapore Embassy received a message from the Kremlin. The message was that a black limousine would pick me up from the embassy and bring me to the Kremlin. I was to go alone. At the appointed hour, a black limousine did pick me up from the Singapore Embassy and brought me to the Kremlin.

When I arrived in the Kremlin, I was received by Mr V P Kuznetsov, Counsellor of the Foreign Ministry. The Kremlin is an inspiring place and a visitor cannot help but be impressed by its scale and grandeur. Mr Kuznetsov escorted me down a long corridor into a meeting room and left me there.

After a while, a good-looking and well-dressed Russian gentleman came in and shook my hand. He spoke good English. His name was S N Krasavchenko, the First Deputy

Head of the Administration of President Yeltsin. My guess was that he was either from the Foreign Service or the KGB (Committee for State Security).

To break the ice, I told him of my admiration for Russian composers and writers. He told me that he had served in Japan and we had a short discussion about Japanese culture.

I then briefed him about my mission. I told him about the outstanding issues in the negotiations between Russia and Estonia and Latvia. I briefly described the compromises I would suggest in my report to the UN General Assembly. He listened and did not ask me any questions. I asked him to brief President Yeltsin and to convey my good wishes to the President. He said that he would do so.

I think my meeting with Mr Krasavchenko, courtesy of Ambassador Pickering, was the critical one in Moscow. President Yeltsin had the final authority on whether to accept compromises. Only the US Ambassador had the clout to bypass the Foreign Ministry and go directly to the Kremlin. I will always be grateful to Ambassador Pickering for his help.

Enjoying dinner at the home of Singapore's Ambassador to Russia Joe Conceicao. Mrs Anita Conceicao is sitting in the middle of the couch.

Meeting with Russia's Deputy Foreign Minister Vitaly Churkin (standing to my right). My delegation and I briefed the Russian delegation on our visits to Estonia, Latvia and Lithuania, reviewed unresolved issues raised by the leaders of those countries, and discussed possible compromises.

Coming to my rescue in securing an appointment with a senior member of Russian President Boris Yeltsin's personal staff is US Ambassador to Russia Tom Pickering.

Awed by the scale and grandeur of the Kremlin.

Greeting me at the Kremlin is V P Kuznetsov, Counsellor of Russia's Foreign Ministry.

Report to the United Nations Secretary-General and the General Assembly

From Moscow, we flew back to New York. I met the United Nations Secretary-General and gave him a brief report on my mission. He expressed satisfaction with my mission and encouraged me to write a good report to the General Assembly.

With the help of my political and military advisers, I proceeded to write my report to the General Assembly. The report, entitled, "Report of the Good Offices Mission to Estonia, Latvia, Lithuania and the Russian Federation", dated 14 September 1993, was circulated to the General Assembly (see Annex B). It was adopted without a vote.

The good news was that the subsequent negotiations between Estonia, Lithuania, Latvia and Russia were successful. Russian troops were withdrawn from Lithuania in 1993 and from Estonia and Latvia in 1994. Since 1994, Russia and its three Baltic neighbours have lived at peace with one another. Although the three Baltic countries are members of the North Atlantic Treaty Organization, they have felt threatened by the Russian invasion of Ukraine. The fear is that, if Russia were to succeed in Ukraine, they could be the next victims.

Chapter 9

Reflections

Thirty-one years have passed since my visits to Estonia, Latvia and Lithuania. I have, however, followed their progress with admiration.

In 2004, all three Baltic countries joined the European Union (EU) and the North Atlantic Treaty Organization (NATO). The EU has been very helpful to them in their economic development. Joining NATO has given them the security and protection they sought.

All three countries have made impressive progress in their economic development. Estonia's per capita income in 1991, when it became independent, was US$3,435. It is now US$45,000. Estonia is admired for being the most digitised country in the world.

In 1991, Latvia's per capita income was US$3,435. It has risen to US$40,000. In the case of Lithuania, it was

US$2,776. It has risen to US$49,245 today. In comparison, Russia's per capita income in 2022 was US$15,000.

It would not be wrong to say that Estonia, Latvia and Lithuania have performed an economic miracle in the last 30 years. They have gone from being poor countries to rich countries. Their future is bright.

I would now like to say a few words about NATO's expansion. Russia has said repeatedly that it has felt threatened by NATO's expansion. It has even used the so-called threat posed by NATO's expansion as an excuse for its invasion of Ukraine. China has endorsed the Russian narrative. Because of China's prestige and influence, many people in the world, including Singaporeans, have accepted the Russian narrative as true.

What is the truth? The truth is that NATO's expansion is driven by demand and not by some wicked plot in Brussels or Washington to threaten Russia. Estonia, Latvia and Lithuania had every reason to fear Russia. In order to protect themselves against any future aggression by Russia, they had applied to join NATO. NATO did not invite them to join it. It is they who wanted to join. The attraction is in Article 5 of the North Atlantic Treaty. This article enshrines the principle of all for one and one for all. If any NATO country is attacked, it will be defended by all the other NATO members.

I want to deal with another argument often used by the defenders of Russia. The argument is that, as a great power, Russia is entitled to have its sphere of influence. Russia's neighbours and countries which were once part of the Russia Empire should remain in the Russian orbit and not be allowed to join the EU or NATO. I think it is an absurd argument. As sovereign and independent countries, Estonia, Latvia and Lithuania are free to decide their destinies. Why should their geography or history deprive them of this right? There is no law or morality which supports the view that countries which were once ruled by Russia must forever live under Russian hegemony.

I am happy to say that Singapore has diplomatic relations with all three countries. Two of them, Estonia and Lithuania, have opened embassies in Singapore.

Annex A

United Nations General Assembly Resolution 47/21

47/21. Complete withdrawal of foreign military forces from the territories of the Baltic States

The General Assembly,

Having considered the item entitled "Complete withdrawal of foreign military forces from the territories of the Baltic States",

Considering that the United Nations, pursuant to the provisions of its Charter, has a major role to play in, and responsibility for, the maintenance of international peace and security,

Recalling with particular satisfaction that independence was restored in Estonia, Latvia and Lithuania through peaceful and democratic means,

Recognizing that the stationing of foreign military forces on the territories of Estonia, Latvia and Lithuania without the required consent of those countries is a problem remaining from the past that must be resolved in a peaceful manner,

Welcoming recent agreements on the complete withdrawal of foreign military forces from the territory of Lithuania,

Welcoming also the bilateral talks on the complete withdrawal of foreign military forces from the territories of Estonia and Latvia,

Concerned about the continuing absence of any agreements for the complete withdrawal of foreign military forces from the territories of Estonia and Latvia,

Taking note of the report of the Secretary-General entitled "An Agenda for Peace", pursuant to the statement of 31 January 1992 adopted at the conclusion of the meeting held by the Security Council at the level of Heads of State and Government,

Mindful that the timely application of preventive diplomacy is the most desirable and efficient means to ease tensions before they result in conflict,

Welcoming the "Helsinki Document 1992 — The Challenges of Change", in particular paragraph 15, agreed upon at the Conference on Security and Cooperation in Europe, held at Helsinki on 9 and 10 July 1992,

Recognizing that the Conference on Security and Cooperation in Europe is a regional arrangement in the sense of Chapter VIII of the Charter of the United Nations, and as such provides an important link between European and global security,

Recognizing also that regional organizations participating in complementary efforts with the United Nations may encourage States outside the region to act supportively,

1. *Expresses support* for the efforts made by the States participating in the Conference on Security and Cooperation in Europe to remove the foreign military forces stationed on the territories of Estonia, Latvia and Lithuania without the required consent of those countries, in a peaceful manner and through negotiations;

2. *Calls upon* the States concerned, in line with the basic principles of international law and in order to prevent any possible conflict, to conclude without delay appropriate agreements, including timetables, for the early, orderly and complete withdrawal of foreign military forces from the territories of Estonia and Latvia;

3. *Urges* the Secretary-General to use his good offices to facilitate the complete withdrawal of foreign military forces from the territories of Estonia, Latvia and Lithuania;

4. *Requests* the Secretary-General to keep Member States informed of progress towards the implementation of the present resolution and to report thereon to the General Assembly at its forty-eighth session;

5. *Decides* to include in the provisional agenda of its forty-eighth session the item entitled "Complete withdrawal of foreign military forces from the territories of the Baltic States".

72nd plenary meeting
25 November 1992

REPORT OF THE GOOD OFFICES MISSION

TO ESTONIA, LATVIA, LITHUANIA AND

THE RUSSIAN FEDERATION

14 September 1993

CONTENTS

		Paragraphs	Page
I.	INTRODUCTION	1 - 17	1
II.	ASSESSMENT	18 - 41	6
III.	RECOMMENDATIONS	42 - 46	15

<u>Annex</u>

List of officials with whom
the delegation met   18

I.   INTRODUCTION

1.   One of the major issues of concern to the Baltic States is
the withdrawal of the armed forces of the former Soviet Union
from Estonia, Latvia and Lithuania. Since the recognition of the
restoration of their independence by Russia, on 24 August 1991,
and by the Soviet Union on 6 September 1991, the Baltic States
had vigorously pressed for the removal of the Soviet (now
Russian) armed forces from their respective territories.

2.   Several rounds of negotiations on this subject had been held
between the delegations of the three Baltic States and the
Russian Federation during 1992 and 1993. The talks came about
following both Russia's declaration, on 16 January 1992, that it
had assumed jurisdiction over the former Soviet troops deployed
in the Baltic States, and the agreement by all four governments
that the issues to be negotiated would be the complete withdrawal
of those troops from the Baltic States, as well as issues
regarding the Russian population, former Soviet property,
transfer of part of weaponry to the three republics and
territorial questions. Despite the general understanding that
the Russian troops should be removed from the region, agreements
on the terms of their withdrawal had not been reached. While the
Baltic States have insisted on immediate withdrawal, Russia
argued that due to the lack of housing and jobs in Russia for the
military personnel who were to be withdrawn, more time is needed
to make a complete withdrawal of its troops.

UN General Assembly resolution 47/21

3.   At the request of Estonia, Latvia and Lithuania, an item on
the complete withdrawal of foreign troops from their territories
was included in the agenda of the forty-seventh session of the UN
General Assembly. The resolution on this question, 47/21, which

was adopted without a vote, <u>inter alia,</u> called upon all States concerned ... "to conclude without delay, appropriate agreement, including timetables, for the early, orderly and complete withdrawal of foreign military forces from the territories of Estonia, Latvia and Lithuania." The General Assembly urged the Secretary-General to use his good offices to facilitate the complete withdrawal of foreign military forces from the territories of Estonia, Latvia and Lithuania. It also requested the Secretary-General to keep Member States informed of progress towards the implementation of the present resolution and to report thereon to the General Assembly at its forty-eighth session.

<u>Appointment of Special Envoy of the Secretary-General</u>

4.   Pursuant to that resolution, the Secretary-General appointed Professor Tommy Koh, Ambassador-at-Large, in the Ministry of Foreign Affairs of Singapore, as his Special Envoy to lead a mission to the Russian Federation, Latvia, Lithuania and Estonia.

<u>Composition of the UN Mission</u>

5.   The good offices mission was undertaken by Ambassador Koh from 29 August to 9 September 1993 and included Mr. Alexandre Matsouka, Political Affairs Officer in the Department of Political Affairs and Colonel Stanislav Hajek a military adviser from the General Staff of the Czech Republic, who joined the mission on its arrival in Moscow and Ms. Lynda Smith as the Secretary of the delegation.

<u>Consultations in New York</u>

6.   Prior to leaving New York, the mission held intensive consultations from 24 to 27 August 1993 with the representatives of Estonia, Latvia, Lithuania and the Russian Federation, as well

as those of Denmark, Finland, Germany, Poland, Sweden and the
USA.

Consultations in Moscow

7.   On Sunday, 29 August, after its arrival in Moscow, the
mission paid a visit to Solnechnogorsk, a military camp outside
Moscow, where it met Lt. Gen. Puzanov, First Deputy Commander of
the Moscow Military District and saw the difficult housing
conditions of troops and their families. These troops had been
withdrawn from Lithuania.

8.   On Monday, 30 August, the mission met with Mr. Glukhov,
Chief of the European Department; Mr. Krylov, Secretary-General,
Chief of Chancellory, Ministry of Foreign Affairs, as well as
with the heads of the Russian teams at the negotiations:
Ambassadors S. Zotov (Latvia), V. Isakov (Lithuania) and
V. Svirin (Estonia). On the same day the mission discussed
various aspects of the question of troop withdrawal with
Col. Gen. B. Gromov, Deputy Minister of Defence.

9.   On Tuesday, 31 August 1993 the mission met Mr. Stepashin,
Chairman of the Commission on Defence and Security of the Russian
Parliament. This mission also held consultations with the
Ambassadors of Belgium, Denmark, Greece and the USA. That
evening, it flew to Lithuania. Upon its arrival in Vilnius, the
mission attended ceremonies to celebrate the departure of the
last Russian combat unit from Lithuania.

Visit to Lithuania

10. In Lithuania, on Wednesday, 1 September 1993, the mission
met with Col. S. Knezys, Chief of Joint Staff, Ministry of
National Defence. It then inspected a military camp from which
the Russian troops had been withdrawn. It also met

with Mr. A. Butkeviecius, Minister of National Defence. That
afternoon, it met the President of the Republic of Lithuania,
H.E. Mr. A. Brazauskas and later, at the Ministry of Foreign
Affairs, with H.E. Mr. Gylys, Minister for Foreign Affairs,
followed by a meeting with Mr. V. Domarkas, Deputy Minister for
Foreign Affairs, and with the Lithuanian negotiating team on
troop withdrawal: Professor Bulovas, Head of the delegation;
Mr. Ozolas and Professor Vadapalas.

11.   On Thursday morning, 2 September 1993 it held a meeting with
representatives of retired Russian war veterans and retirees and
met with the diplomatic corps in Lithuania. In the afternoon, it
met with the Chairman of Parliament, Mr. C. Jursenas.

Visit to Latvia

12.   On Friday, 3 September 1993, the mission travelled by
motorcade to Latvia. In the afternoon it met with
H.E. G. Ulmanis, the President of the Republic of Latvia. Later,
official talks were held in the Ministry of Foreign Affairs with
H.E. Professor G. Andrejevs, Minister for Foreign Affairs;
followed by a meeting with the Latvian team at the negotiations
with the Russian Federation: The Hon. M. Virsis, Head of the
delegation; Mr. A. Vovers, Undersecretary for Eastern Issues;
Col. D. Turlais, Commander of Defence Forces, Ministry of Defence
and Mr. M. Supe, President's Adviser for Foreign Affairs. Later
that evening it held a meeting with the Dean of the Diplomatic
Corps., H.E. H. Count Lambsdorf of Germany.

13.   On Saturday, 4 September 1993, in the morning, meetings were
held at the Saeima (Parliament) with: Ms. I. Birzniece, MP,
Chairman, Saeima Standing Committee for Human Rights;
Mr. A. Kirsteins, MP, Chairman, Saeima Foreign Relations Standing
Committee; Mr. I. Silars, MP, Chairman, Saeima Defence and
Interior Affairs Standing Committee and Mr. A. Pantelejevs, MP,

Chairman, Saeima Standing Committee on National Security.
Subsequently, the mission met with Lt. Gen. Melnichuk, Deputy
Commander of the North-West Military Group and with retired
Russian military officers in Latvia.

Visit to Liepaja and Skrunda

14.   On Sunday, 5 September, the mission flew by a Latvian
military aircraft to Liepaja to inspect the Russian naval base.
It was accompanied by Mr. I. Upmalis, Head of the Control Bureau
on the Withdrawal of Russian Armed Forces, MFA; Captain Stalev,
Commander of the base and Mr. I. Vismins, Mayor of Liepaja. The
mission also visited another Russian strategic installation in
Latvia - an ABM early-warning radar station at Skrunda. That
evening it flew to Estonia.

Visit to Estonia

15.   The following morning, 6 September, it met with Mr. J. Luik,
Minister of Defence, Head of the Estonian delegation,
Mr. T. Velliste, Minister of Foreign Affairs and Mr. A. Tarand,
Minister of the Environment. This was followed by a meeting with
the Speaker of the Estonian Parliament, Mr. U. Nugis and
Mr. Saatpalu, Chairman of the Foreign Affairs Committee of the
Parliament. In the afternoon, it met with representatives
Russian World War II veterans and retirees, and with the
diplomatic corps. A meeting was also held with
Ambassador T. Lahelma, Head of the CSCE Human Rights mission to
Estonia.

Visit to Paldiski

16.   The next day, 7 September the mission met the Estonian Prime
Minister, Mr. M. Laar followed by a meeting with

- 6 -

H.E. Mr. A. Trofimov, Ambassador of the Russian Federation. It
then travelled by car to inspect a Russian submarine training
centre at Paldiski. Before departing Estonia the mission met
with Major-General Mr. A. Einseln, General Commander of the
Estonian Defence Forces. This was followed by a meeting with
H.E. Mr. L. Meri, the President of the Republic of Estonia.
Later that afternoon the mission departed for Moscow.

Return to Moscow

17. On Wednesday, 8 September 1993, the mission met again with
the Heads of the Russian delegations. Later, it was received by
the Deputy Foreign Minister, V. Churkin, and also met with
Mr. Y.E. Fokine, Head of the Second European Department, MFA. In
the afternoon it met the Ambassadors of the three Baltic States
in Moscow. That evening, the Special Envoy met with
Mr. S. Krasavchenko, First Deputy Head of the Administration of
the President of the Russian Federation.

II. ASSESSMENT

18. Russian officials had confirmed their readiness to withdraw
their remaining troops from Estonia and ~~Lithuania~~ Latvia. The only
outstanding issue was the terms and conditions of their
withdrawal and the satisfactory resolution of some related
issues. Since 1992, Russia had withdrawn most of its combat
units from the Baltic States. However, since the remaining
troops in Estonia and Latvia were among the last to be brought
back to Russia from the former Republics of the Soviet Union and
other countries in Eastern Europe, the need to find adequate
housing for them was particularly acute. The question of troop
withdrawal had become a domestic political issue in all the
countries concerned.

Lithuania

19.   The last Russian combat unit was withdrawn from Lithuania on
31 August 1993.   There are now only a few hundred unarmed Russian
troops left to take care of the military hospitals and other
administrative details.   These will be withdrawn shortly.
Therefore, as far as Lithuania is concerned, the objective of
General Assembly resolution 47/21, has almost been achieved.
There is no need for the Secretary-General to exercise his good
offices to assist the governments of the Russian Federation and
Lithuania to resolve the two remaining issues, i.e., the status
and social benefits of Russian veterans and retirees and the
right of transit by Russia through Lithuania to Kaliningrad
Oblast.   Lithuania was the only Baltic country in which we met
Russian military pensioners who expressed a desire to return to
Russia and who complained bitterly about the failure of their
government to assist them to do so.

Estonia

20.   In the case of Estonia, the number of Russian troops
remaining was estimated by various Russian officials at between
5,000 to 6,000.   There had been no agreement between Russia and
Estonia on the deadline for the total withdrawal of these troops.
Unlike the case of Lithuania, Russia would not agree to withdraw
its remaining troops until a binding legal agreement had been
agreed upon.   Estonia had accepted this condition provided, of
course, that the substance of the agreement was acceptable.
Russia had also insisted on linking the date of withdrawal with
two other related issues:

    (a)   the status and social benefits of Russian veterans and
retirees; and

    (b)   an agreement on Paldiski.

- 8 -

Date of withdrawal

21. Regarding the date of withdrawal, the Estonians would like
all Russian troops to be withdrawn before the end of 1993,
preferably before Christmas. Russia has offered to withdraw its
troops by the end of 1994. The Russian side has explained that,
although the number of troops to be withdrawn was not large, the
accommodation for the troops based in Tallinn and their families
has not yet been built in the town of Smolensk which has been
chosen as their destination. The Government of Estonia has
expressed a willingness to participate in a multinational effort
to build housing for returning troops and their families.

Russian veterans and retirees

22. The second issue concerns the status and social benefits of
Russian veterans and retirees. The President of the Union of
Veterans and Pensioners, Retired Colonel Belozerov, informed us
that there were approximately 52,000 veterans and retirees. The
veterans and retirees informed us that they would like to
continue to reside in Estonia. They fear that Article 12,
paragraph 4, sub-paragraph 7 of the Law on Aliens could lead to
their expulsion. This sub-paragraph reads:

> "(4) A residence permit shall not be issued to an
>   alien:
>
>   (7) who has served in a career position in the
>   armed forces of a foreign State or has
>   entered the reserve forces or has retired from
>   a career position in the armed forces of a
>   foreign State, nor to his or her family
>   members, who have entered Estonia in
>   conjunction with the service or retirement
>   of a member of such armed forces."

23.   The Prime Minister of Estonia informed us that a decree is
being prepared to implement the Law on Aliens. The decree would
exempt all persons over the age of 60. Those below the age of 60
would be treated on a case-by-case basis and certain individuals,
for example, those who had acted against the Estonian state and
its security would be denied residence permits.

24.   I informed the Prime Minister that persons who had acted
against the Estonian State and its security and other
objectionable persons had already been dealt with by other sub-
paragraphs, for example, (2), (3), (4) and (5). I recommended
to the Prime Minister to consider a cut-off date, such as, the
date on which Estonia regained its independence and all those who
retired before the cut-off date should be entitled to residence
permits. I told the representatives of the Russian veterans and
retirees that, on the one hand, they could no longer expect to
enjoy special rights and privileges but, on the other hand, they
should not be discriminated against and should be treated with
fairness and humanity. If they wanted to become Estonian
citizens they must be loyal to Estonia, learn its language and
respect its culture.

<u>Paldiski</u>

25.   The <u>third</u> issue concerned Paldiski where there was an
important submarine training centre which has been shut down.
There are two nuclear-powered submarines at the centre. The
nuclear reactors had been deactivated, but the question which
divided the two sides concerned the amount of time it would take
for the Russian authorities to remove the nuclear fuel rods from
the two reactors, to remove the nuclear waste in storage, to
remove the reactors and other military secrets and to clean up
the site ecologically. The Estonian government had built a rail
link to Paldiski which would make it possible to ship the
reactors and nuclear materials by rail to St. Petersburg. The

two submarines are located in a building 4 kilometres from the
port. It might be feasible to bring the submarines to the port
and tow them to St. Petersburg.

26. In any case, the Estonians believed that it would take only
a few months for the Russians to remove the nuclear fuel rods,
nuclear reactors and other military equipment. If necessary, the
Estonian government was prepared to consider the possibility of
asking for the help of IAEA and friendly governments, such as
Sweden, to help with the nuclear-decontamination of Paldiski. On
the other hand, the Russians told us in Moscow and Paldiski, that
the task could not be completed before 1996 and 1999
respectively.

Conclusion

27. I am reasonably optimistic that a fair and balanced
agreement(s) between Estonia and Russia, embracing all three
elements, can be arrived at. On the date of withdrawal, a
compromise between the two options is feasible. On the status
and social benefits of Russian veterans and retirees, the Russian
side should be satisfied if Estonia accepted the suggestions I
put forward to its Prime Minister concerning the decree being
formulated to implement the Law on Aliens. As for Paldiski, the
issue is, in essence, technical and not political. An earlier
date for the withdrawal of the troops from Estonia, especially
those in Tallinn, would probably enable Estonia to be more
flexible on other issues. On Paldiski, given goodwill on both
sides and a willingness to accommodate each other, I am confident
that a practical solution can be worked out, within a much
shorter time-frame than those suggested by the Russian side.

Latvia

28.   The Russians and Latvians had agreed to negotiate a legally
binding agreement providing for the troop withdrawal from Latvia.
So far, the two sides had not been able to agree on a date.
Latvia would like all Russian troops to leave their territory
before the end of 1993.   Russia had offered the end of 1994.   The
Russians explained that they needed the longer period because of
the acute shortage of housing in Russia to accommodate the
returnees and because there were 18,000 troops left in Latvia.

29.   Russia wanted a package deal, consisting of an agreed date
for troop withdrawal, agreement on the status and social benefits
of Russian veterans and retirees, and agreement(s) on three
"strategic" facilities in Skrunda, Venspils and Liepaja.

Date of withdrawal

30.   The date for the withdrawal of Russian troops from Latvia is
politically and psychologically important to the Latvians.   The
Russian side should try to understand this and should try to
agree to an earlier date, taking into account the logistical
realities of finding accommodation in Russia for the 18,000
troops and their families.   The Latvian side and the
international community could help by accelerating the process of
building housing in Russia for the returnees.

No citizenship law

31.   The issue of the status and social benefits of Russian
veterans and retirees in Latvia was difficult for a number of
reasons.   Russia's chief negotiator, Ambassador Zotov, informed
us that there were approximately 20,000 Russian military
pensioners in Latvia.   He said that 87% of them would like to
become Latvian citizens.   Latvia had not yet enacted a

citizenship law. Before doing so, it is my hope that Latvia will take into account the views and recommendations of the UN fact-finding mission, the Council of Europe and the CSCE and act expeditiously on the matter.

Russian veterans and retirees

32. I was informed by the Latvian Chairman of the Parliamentary Committee on Human Rights, Ms. Inese Birzniece, that there were two draft agreements on the status and social benefits of Russian veterans and retirees. According to Ms. Birzniece, there were four or five outstanding points in the two draft agreements.

33. One outstanding point was the cut-off date separating those retirees who were entitled to permanent residence and those who were not. The Latvian side had proposed 4 May 1990 as the cut-off date. The Russian side had counter-proposed 28 January 1992, the day on which negotiations began. The 4th of May 1990, the day on which Latvia gained or regained its independence would seem a more logical cut-off date.

34. The second issue concerned property rights. At present, only co-operative apartments built after 1940 could be privatised. There was a seven year period during which former owners of such apartments could file claims against their present owners. This meant that the Russian owners of such apartments would have to wait seven years before they could sell them. Other apartments could not be sold because of a legal vacuum. I advised Ms. Birzniece that the Latvian Parliament should enact, as expeditiously as possible, a general law on the privatisation of apartments.

35. The third issue concerned medicare. Many of the veterans and retirees are elderly people. They were naturally concerned about their access to healthcare after the departure of Russian

troops and the closure of Russian military hospitals. One
possible solution would be to follow the Lithuanian example and
accord to the Russian veterans and retirees the same medicare as
for Latvian citizens.

36. The fourth issue concerned the fear expressed by some
veterans and retirees that they would be discriminated against.
Ms. Birzniece assured me that a law would be passed to ensure
that the Russian veterans and retirees would be treated equally
with Latvian citizens and other residents. In addition, she said
she would propose the creation of an ombudsman and a consultative
council on nationalities under the Ministry of Justice.

Strategic facilities

37. Russia's three "strategic facilities" in Latvia constitute
another difficult item on the negotiating agenda.

Liepaja

38. Russia had described the naval base at Liepaja as a
strategic facility. Russia had requested Latvia a special
agreement which would enable her to retain Liepaja for a period
of five to six years after the date of troop withdrawal. We were
able to visit the port and naval base and observed them for
ourselves. We were unimpressed and not convinced of its
strategic value to Russia. Our impression was confirmed by the
Commander of the base, Captain Stalev, who informed us that a
time-table for the withdrawal of the Russian Navy from Liepaja by
the end of 1994 had been drawn up by the Commander of the Baltic
Fleet. What Russia wanted thereafter was for Russian warships
and merchant ships to have the right to visit the port and enjoy
the use of its facilities.

- 14 -

<u>Skrunda</u>

39.   Next, we visited Skrunda. The Russians had built at
Skrunda, in the 1960s, an anti-ballistic missile early warning
system. According to its Commander, Skrunda covered a segment of
the sky which was not covered by any other ABM early warning
system in Russia or Ukraine. Therefore, he argued that if
Skrunda were shut down, it would leave a hole in the sky. For
this reason, Russia requested Latvia to consider a special lease
agreement, whereunder, Russia would compensate Latvia for being
allowed to continue to operate this facility. Russia said that
it would need eight to ten years to build a facility inside
Russian territory to replace Skrunda. In the phasing-out period,
Russia was prepared to consider training Latvians to operate the
facility, in the same way that they had done in Ukraine and
Kazakstan. The Latvians were not sympathetic to the Russian
request. They doubted the veracity of the Russian statements
concerning the strategic significance of Skrunda to Russia's
national security. They suspected that the segment of the sky
covered by Skrunda was also covered by other ABM early warning
stations. They would only consider the retention of the facility
at Skrunda if it came under international control. The gap
between Russia and Latvia over Skrunda was wide and it would not
be easy to bridge it.

<u>Venspils</u>

40.   Owing to the shortage of time, we were unable to visit the
facility at Venspils. According to Russia, the facility at
Venspils was to monitor space objects. According to Latvia, it
was to eavesdrop on communications in Northern Europe, especially
among the Scandinavian countries. There was therefore a dispute
between the two sides over the nature of the facility and its
strategic significance, if any, to Russia. Russia had requested
Latvia to consider a lease agreement for a period of six years.

It would help the negotiation on Venspils if we were able to
obtain an objective and authoritative assessment of the nature of
the facility, its strategic significance to Russia, if any, and
the time it would take for Russia to replicate such a facility
(if it was in fact needed) on Russian territory.

Conclusion

41.   Although the negotiations between Latvia and Russia were
difficult, it would still be possible for them to reach an
acceptable agreement(s) on all the three issues if the two sides
had the political will to agree, if Latvia were prepared to put
its painful past behind it, if Russia were prepared to treat
Latvia as a sovereign and independent State, and if both
countries shared the vision of building a new future based on
equality, mutual benefit and good neighbourliness. The Russian
veterans and retirees who wished to remain in Latvia, like those
in Estonia, must be prepared to make the necessary psychological,
linguistic and cultural changes. The continued presence of
Russian combat troops in the capital of Latvia, Riga, is
politically and pyscologically offensive to the Latvians. An
early withdrawal of these troops from Riga would be interpreted
by the Latvians as a gesture of goodwill.

III.   RECOMMENDATIONS

42. First, we commend Estonia, Latvia, Lithuania, Denmark,
Norway, the United States of America and other countries for
joining in a multinational effort to help Russia build housing
for the troops and their families returning from the three Baltic
countries. Obviously, the faster this housing programme could be
implemented, the sooner would Russia be able to withdraw its
remaining troops from Estonia and Latvia. We had seen with our
own eyes the difficult housing conditions for troops and their
families who had been withdrawn from the Baltic region. The

housing problem of returning troops and their families is therefore a real one.

43.   Second, in the forthcoming weeks and months, the countries concerned should refrain from making any statements or actions which are provocative or unfriendly toward one another. Instead, they should make goodwill gestures towards one another in order to improve the negotiating atmosphere and prospects.

44.   Third, countries which are friendly to both sides, such as the Scandinavian countries, USA, EC, and international organizations, such as the CSCE and the Council of Europe, should continue to use their benign influence and help to resolve the remaining questions.

45.   Fourth, Estonia and Russia would be holding their next round of negotiations on the 14th and 15th of September. Let us hope that they succeed. In the event that they do not, I recommend that the Secretary-General invite them to send negotiators to New York, at the level of ministers or deputy ministers, for negotiations on the 30th of September and 1st of October. The negotiations would be chaired by a representative of the Secretary-General. If the need should arise,
the Secretary-General could intervene to resolve any sticking point in the negotiations.

46.   Fifth, Latvia and Russia would also be holding their next round of negotiations on the 27th and 28th of September. We must also hope that they will succeed. However, in the event that they did not, I recommend that the Secretary-General invite them to send negotiators to New York, at the level of ministers or deputy ministers, for negotiations on the 4th and 5th of October. The negotiations would be chaired by a representative of the Secretary-General. Again, if the need should arise, the

- 17 -

Secretary-General could intervene to resolve any sticking point
in the negotiations.

                                        Tommy Koh
                                        14 September 1993

- 18 -

Annex
LIST OF OFFICIALS WITH WHOM THE DELEGATION MET

MOSCOW

H.E. S.N. Krasavchenko, First Deputy Head of the Administration
   of the President of the Russian Federation
Mr. Stepashin, Chairman of the Commission on Defence and Security
   of the Russian Parliament
V. Churkin, Deputy Foreign Minister
Col. Gen. Gromov, Deputy Minister of Defence
Lt. Gen. Puzanov, First Deputy Commander of
   the Moscow Military District
Mr. S.B. Krylov, Executive Secretary,
   Ministry of Foreign Affairs
Mr. Glukhov, Chief of European Directorate,
   Ministry of Foreign Affairs
Mr. Y.E. Fokine, Head of the Second European Department,
   Ministry of Foreign Affairs
Mr. S. S. Zotov, Head of the Russian State delegation at the
   negotiations with Latvia
Mr. V. Isakov, Head of the Russian State delegation at the
   negotiations with Lithuania
Mr. V. Svirin, Head of the Russian State delegation at the
   negotiations with Estonia
Mr. V. P. Kuznetsov, Counsellor MFA, Russian Federation

LITHUANIA

H.E. Mr. A. Brazauskas, President of the Republic of Lithuania
Mr. C. Jursenas, Chairman of Parliament
Mr. A. Butkeviecius, Minister of National Defence,
   Ministry of National Defence
H.E. Mr. Gylys, Minister for Foreign Affairs
Col. S. Knezys, Chief of Joint Staff, Ministry of
   National Defence
Mr. V. Domarkas, Deputy Minister, Minister for Foreign Affairs,
Professor V. V. Bulovas, Head of the Lithuanian delegation at the
   negotiations with the Russian Federation
Mr. R. Ozolas, Member of the Lithuanian delegation at the
   negotiations with the Russian Federation
Professor V. Vadapalas, Member of the Lithuanian delegation at
   the negotiations with the Russian Federation

<u>LATVIA</u>

H.E. G. Ulmanis, President of the Republic of Latvia
Ms. I. Birzniece, MP, Chairman,
  Saeima Standing Committee for Human Rights
Mr. A. Kirsteins, MP, Chairman,
  Saeima Foreign Relations Standing Committee
Mr. I. Silars, MP, Chairman,
  Saeima Defence and Interior Affairs Standing Committee
Mr. A. Pantelejevs, MP, Chairman,
  Saeima Standing Committee on National Security
H.E. Professor G. Andrejevs, Minister of Foreign Affairs
The Hon. M. Virsis, Head of the Latvian delegation at the
  negotiations with the Russian Federation
Mr. A. Vovers, Undersecretary for Eastern Issues,
  Member of the Latvian delegation at the negotiations
  with the Russian Federation
Col. D. Turlais, Commander of Defence Forces,
  Ministry of Defence
  Member of the Latvian delegation at the negotiations
  with the Russian Federation
Mr. M. Supe, President's Adviser for Foreign Affairs
  Member of the Latvian delegation at the negotiations
  with the Russian Federation
Mr. I. Upmalis, Head of Control Bureau on the
  Withdrawal of Russian Armed Forces, Ministry of Foreign Affairs
Mr. I. Vismins, Mayor of Liepaja
H.E. H. Count Lambsdorf, Ambassador of Germany
  The Dean of the Diplomatic Corps
Lt. Gen. Melnichuk, Deputy Commander of the North-West
  Military Group of the Armed Forces of the Russian Federation
Captain Stalev, Commander of the Liepaja Naval base

<u>ESTONIA</u>

H.E. Mr. L. Meri, the President of the Republic of Estonia
Mr. M. Laar, Prime Minister of the Republic of Estonia
Mr. U. Nugis, Speaker of the Estonian Parliament
Mr. Saatpalu, Chairman of the Foreign Affairs Committee
  of the Parliament
Mr. J. Luik, Minister of Defence
Major-General Mr. A. Einseln, General Commander of
  the Estonian Defence Forces
Mr. T. Velliste, Minister of Foreign Affairs
Mr. A. Tarand, Minister of the Environment
Mr. A. Ollium, General Secretary, Ministry of Foreign Affairs

– 20 –

Mr. T. Miller, Chief of Division, Political Department,
   Ministry of Foreign Affairs
Ambassador Timo Lahelma, Head of CSCE
   Human Rights Mission to Estonia
H.E. Mr. A. Trofimov, Ambassador of the Russian Federation

Index

A
Aliens Law, 29
Andrejevs, Georgs, 19
anti-ballistic missile, 21

B
Baltic country, 4, 7, 33, 42
Birzniece, I., 20
Boutros-Ghali, Boutros, 6, 8
Brazauskas, Algirdas, 13–14
Bulovas, V. V., 15
Burma, 27
Burmese Chief of Protocol, 27

C
Chief of Protocol of Lithuania, 13
Churkin, Vitaly, 33, 37

"Comrade Boris", 14
Conceicao, Anita, 36
Conceicao, Joe, 36
Conference on Security and Cooperation, 48
Cuéllar, Javiér Perez de, 6

E
Earth Summit, 8
Einseln, Aleksander, 25
Estonia, 2–4, 25–32, 43–45, 51–63
European Union, 43, 45

F
First World War, 2
Fokine, Y. E., 18, 33
foreign military forces, 47–49

G
Gromov, Boris, 11–12

H
Hajek, Stanislav, 9–10, 12
Hitler–Stalin pact, xviii

I
Isakov, Virgilijus, 11, 18

K
Kirsteins, A., 20
Koh, Paul Kok Hong, 10, 16
Krasavchenko, S. N., 34–35
Krylov, Boris Nikolaevich, 11
Kuznetsov, V. P., 34, 39

L
Laar, Mart, 25, 29
Landsbergis, Vytautas, 13
Latvia, 1–4, 19–23, 43–45, 51–63
Latvians, 21
Law of Aliens, 29
Liepaja, 20–21
Lithuania, 1–4, 13–18, 45, 51–63
Luik, Jüri, 25
Lustig, Fredrich V., 27

M
Matsuoka, Alexandre, 9–10, 12

Meri, Lennart, 25, 31
Miller, T., 26
Moscow, 1, 9–12, 33–39

N
Nevsky, Alexander, 32
North Atlantic Treaty Organization, 43–45
Nugis, Ülo, 26

O
Ozolas, R., 15

P
Pantelejevs, A., 20
Parliament Square, 13
Pickering, Tom, 11, 34–35, 38
Puzanov, Igor, 10

R
Resolution 47/5, 21–6
Riga, 22
Russia, 1–2, 20, 26, 41, 45

S
Second World War, 1
Secretary-General, 49
Siberia, 3, 25, 27, 31
Silars, I., 20
Singapore, xv, xxi, 3, 6, 34, 45
Skrunda, 21

Smith, Lynda, 9
Soviet delegation, 27
Soviet Union, 1–2, 28
Special Envoy, 6–7
Stepashin, Sergei, 11
Supe, M., 19
Svirin, Vasili, 11, 18

T
Tarand, Andres, 25
Turlais, D., 19

U
UN General Assembly, 5, 35, 41–42
Union of Soviet Socialist Republics, 1–2

United Kingdom, 1, 9, 12
United Nations, 5–7, 9
United Nations Secretary-General, 41–42
United States, xiv, 1, 10, 34

V
Velliste, Trivimi, 25
Virsis, M., 19
Vovers, A., 19

Y
Yeltsin, Boris, 14, 38

Z
Zotov, Sergei, 11, 18